THE CREATIVE BOOK OF

Flower Crafts

Flower Crafts

Joanna Sheen

Published by Salamander Books Limited
LONDON • NEW YORK

Published by Salamander Books Ltd.,
129-137 York Way,
London N7 9LG,
United Kingdom.

©Salamander Books Ltd. 1992

ISBN 0 86101 669 6

Distributed in Canada by Cavendish Books Inc.,
Unit 5, 801 West 1st Street,
North Vancouver, B.C. V7P 1A4.
Phone (604) 985-2969.

—————— *CREDITS* ——————

Managing Editor: Jane Struthers

Art Director: Roger Daniels

Editor: Felicity Jackson

Photographer: Jon Stewart, assisted by Sandra Lambell

Indexer: William Martin

Typeset by: BMD Graphics, Hemel Hempstead

Colour origination by: Regent Publishing Services

Printed in Belgium by: Proost International Book Division

CONTENTS

INTRODUCTION

Flowers can be a constant source of pleasure, and an added bonus when you dry or press flowers is their extended life. In this book there are many beautiful gift ideas that will delight friends and relatives or you can even make them for yourself. All the projects shown in the following chapters are simple to make, providing you follow the instructions carefully. They will bring hours of pleasure to the recipient, and you will have a lot of fun making them as well! The raw materials can either be bought, or harvested from your own garden or that of a friend. Alternatively, keep your eyes open when walking in the countryside, where there are often fallen cones or nuts you can use in your craft work.

Silk flowers are always interesting to work with, they don't fade or droop and a wonderful selection is available from department stores and smaller craft shops or florists. Although they are fairly expensive, it only takes a few blooms to make something really eye-catching, so they can be a worthwhile investment.

Also included are some ideas for using flowers in the kitchen. Edible flowers are slowly gaining in popularity, although they are an acquired taste! However, the selection of teas, vinegars and honey would all be very acceptable as a gift or on the family breakfast table.

Hopefully the dozens of ideas contained in this book will inspire you to think of many more and to use your own artistic ability (yes, we all have some somewhere!) to create even more original and wonderful gifts and crafts.

───── PRESERVING FLOWERS ─────

M any of the projects in this book use preserved flowers that have been pressed, dried or preserved in silica gel crystals, and the techniques are explained fully on these pages.

PRESSED FLOWERS
Garden and wild flowers can all be pressed with a minimum amount of equipment and by following a few simple instructions. Choose fairly flat flowers, not thick-centred, multi-petalled blooms. Pick the flowers when they are completely dry – about mid-morning on a dry day. Only harvest really fresh, new flowers – if you put rubbish into a press you will get rubbish out.

A flower press can be bought from a craft shop or department store and consists of 2 pieces of wood with holes drilled in each corner. A set of 4 bolts are inserted through the holes and a screw fitting placed on the end of each bolt. The contents of the press should be 20 pieces of good quality blotting paper interspersed with thick pads of newspaper. If you buy a press and there are pieces of card inside, throw them away and replace with newspapers.

Having picked some fresh, dry material, you need to place it in the press. Open the press and place some newspaper on the bottom, then put a sheet of blotting paper on top. The flowers should have any stalks or pieces that stick out unnecessarily trimmed off, then the flowers can be placed on the blotting paper, with space between each flower or leaf. Cover this layer with another sheet of blotting paper and then some more newspaper. Continue to build up the layers in the press until you have used all the papers. Screw down the press tightly and label with the date and contents. The press should then be put in a warm dry place and left for about 6 weeks. After that time the flowers will be ready to use and can be removed from the press.

DRYING FLOWERS
There is a wide variety of flowers you can preserve by drying, and the the easiest way is to air dry them. This produces the most robust finished product, one that will last better in changes of temperature and will be less brittle to handle. To air dry flowers, make up small bunches – usually about 5 stems at a time – and bunch together with an elastic band placed about 2.5 cm (1 in) down the stems.

Hang the bunches upside down in a warm, ventilated room with as little natural light as possible. It usually takes from about a week to a month for the flowers to dry, depending on the ambient temperature and the variety of flower. Once the bunches are dry, they can be stored in a tissue-lined florist's box, away from harmful sunlight and damp. Dried flowers keep well but it is usually advisable to use them within a year for them to be at their best.

POT POURRI INGREDIENTS
Pot pourri can include almost anything you choose, as you will see from the recipes that follow. If you want to dry leaves or flowers very rapidly for use in pot pourri, they can be dried in a conventional oven or in a microwave. Their shape will distort and often the colour alters but this does not matter when they are destined for a pot pourri mix. It is still wise to choose prime materials for drying but you can also use petals or flower heads that have dropped off your arrangements or fallen while they have been hanging up to dry. The ingredients that are

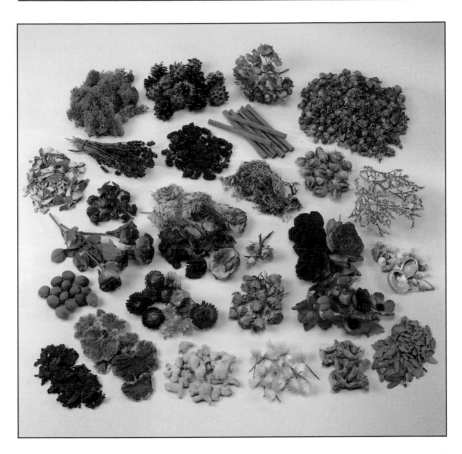

harder to find, such as orris root or unusual spices, can be obtained by mail order from several firms and these are listed at the back of the book. Likewise, the oils are usually available from many high street outlets (check before buying that they are essential oils and not blends of oils) but if you have difficulty locating the exact fragrance that you want, then there are mail order sources that may be able to help.

DRYING IN SILICA GEL CRYSTALS

To obtain perfect results when drying individual flowers, silica gel crystals are the answer. These crystals remove the moisture from the plant materials but keep the colour and shape perfectly, making them particularly useful for decorating the top of a mix of pot pourri. The crystals may be available from your local florist or garden centre; if not, try one of the mail order sources listed at the back of the book. The crystals are expensive but can be used many, many times.

The crystals often come in a plastic container, and this can be used for the drying process. Empty the crystals into a bowl and then spoon some back into the bottom of the plastic container to a depth of about 2.5 cm (1 in). Stand flower heads in the 2.5 cm (1 in) of crystals and, with a teaspoon, carefully cover them with more crystals, filling every crevice and gap until they are completely buried. Place the lid on the box and leave them for about a week, then carefully unpack them with a teaspoon, taking care not to damage the very brittle flowers. The dried flowers should be stored in an airtight container with a few crystals to keep them free from damp. To discourage any reabsorption of moisture, you can spray the flowers with some light polyurethane varnish. You can only dry the flower heads so a false stem will have to be wired on should you wish to use the flower in an arrangement.

ROSE POT POURRI

A gorgeous, traditional fragrance to perfume any room in the house, this pot pourri also makes a stunning decoration. You will need 15 ml (1 tbsp) each of dried red rose petals, lavender, pink rosebuds and dried orange peel, 4 or 5 broken cinnamon sticks, 5 ml (1 tsp) orris root powder, 15 drops rose essential oil and some dried whole roses for decoration.

Place all the ingredients, except the oil and whole roses, in a bowl and mix with a metal spoon. Do not use a plastic or wooden spoon as it will absorb the oil. Add the 15 drops of essential oil and gently mix again until all the oil is absorbed into the mixture. Put the pot pourri into a polythene bag and seal tightly, then leave to mature for 2 weeks, shaking occasionally.

Empty the mixture into the bowl that you want to use for the display, then decorate the top with some whole roses that have been air dried or, better still, dried in silica gel crystals. (For instructions on silica gel crystals and air drying, see pages 8-9.) The mixture can be revived when necessary by adding more oil and stirring well.

GERANIUM POT POURRI

T his subtle and aromatic pot pourri is especially suitable for a kitchen or dining room. You will need a handful of each of the following dried ingredients: scented geranium leaves, marjoram and oregano flowers, mint leaves and flowers, and blue cornflowers. You will also need 15 ml (1 tbsp) orris root powder and 15 drops rose geranium essential oil.

Remove the stalks from all the flowers and leaves, then gently mix together the ingredients in a bowl. Add the orris root powder and mix again. Finally, add the drops of rose geranium essential oil and mix well until all the oil has been absorbed. Put the mixture into a polythene bag and seal well. Leave for 2 weeks, shaking occasionally.

When the pot pourri has matured, shake well before turning it out of the bag into the container of your choice. Place some of the large, more interesting pieces on top of the bowl as a decoration.

This gaily coloured pot pourri smells just as good as it looks! You will need the following ingredients: 1 cup dried marigold flowers, 4 or 5 broken cinnamon sticks, 15 ml (1 tbsp) each of cloves, star anise and allspice berries and 30 ml (2 tbsp) dried small green leaves, 15 ml (1 tbsp) orris root powder and 12 drops of cinnamon or allspice essential oil.

Place the marigolds, spices and leaves in a mixing bowl and, using a metal spoon, mix them together gently. Add the orris root powder and mix it carefully with the other ingredients.

Drop in the oil and mix until it has been absorbed. Place the mixture in a polythene bag and seal. Allow it to mature for 2 weeks, shaking occasionally, then empty it into a suitable container. You can either decorate the pot pourri with pieces of cinnamon and marigolds or with roses that have been air dried or dried in silica gel crystals (see pages 8-9).

──── SEA SHELL POT POURRI ────

The shells can be collected from the beach, or you can buy shells from many craft shops. You will need the following ingredients: 1 cup assorted shells, a handful oak moss, 6 cinnamon sticks, 1 cup dried blue larkspur flowers, nigella seed heads and beech masts, 30 ml (2 tbsp) orris root powder and 20-30 drops of any essential oil of your choice.

Place all the ingredients, except the orris root powder and oil, in a mixing bowl and mix well together. Add the orris root powder and mix in well. Finally, add 20-30 drops of the oil of your choice and mix in well with a metal spoon until it is completely absorbed.

Place the mixture in a polythene bag and seal for 2 weeks, shaking occasionally. To display the finished pot pourri, remove some of the prettiest shells from the bag, then turn the mixture into your container and arrange the shells on the top. If you have any small star fish or sea horses they would look lovely placed on the top as well.

This pot pourri can easily be made from garden flowers. The mixture illustrated uses the following ingredients: 30 ml (2 tbsp) each of dried pink larkspur, nigella seed heads, white everlasting daisies, small green leaves, pink roses, red rose petals and lavender. You will also need 30 ml (2 tbsp) orris root powder and 15–20 drops carnation essential oil.

Place all the flowers in a mixing bowl and mix gently. Add the orris root powder and carnation oil and mix thoroughly with a metal spoon.

Put the mixture into a polythene bag and seal. Leave for 2 weeks, shaking the bag occasionally. When the pot pourri has matured, turn it out into the container you have chosen and decorate the top with carnations dried in silica gel crystals (see page 9) or any other flower of your choice.

C hristmas is a time for exciting smells and this pot pourri would be perfect for the hall or living room to greet your guests. The ingredients used here are: 2 handfuls assorted cones, 1 cup smallish nuts, 6 cinnamon sticks, 1 cup peeled root ginger, 1 handful dried orange peel, 15 ml (1 tbsp) star anise, 2 or 3 cracked nutmegs and some gold sprayed nigella seed heads or cones.

Mix all the above ingredients together, except the gold seed heads or cones, and add 30 ml (2 tbsp) orris root powder. Then add 10 drops allspice oil, 10 drops ginger oil and 15 drops sweet orange essential oil. Mix all these in thoroughly with a metal spoon.

Place the mixture in a polythene bag and seal for 2 weeks, giving the bag a shake occasionally. Once the mixture is ready, place in a suitably festive container and decorate the top with the gilded nigella seed heads or cones and place in position. If it is placed near a fire or warm radiator, the heat will encourage the perfume to waft around the room.

–LAVENDER AND HERB SACHET–

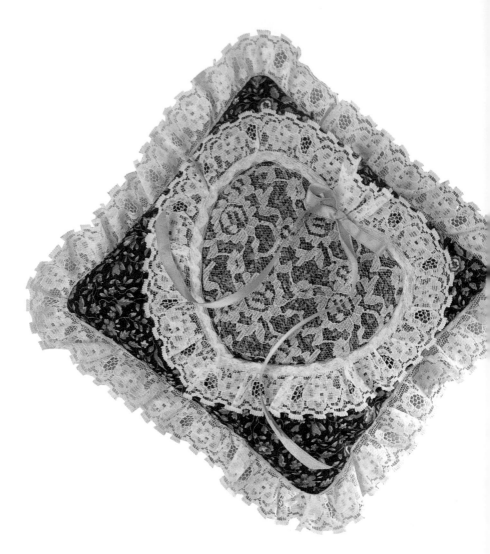

C ut out 2 pieces of cotton fabric and one piece of lace, all about 18 cm (7 in) square. You will also need some dried lavender flowers and leaves, and some dried herbs.

Cut out a heart shape, using the template on page 90, from the middle of one of the pieces of cotton fabric.

Back, with the lace, the piece of cotton fabric with the heart cut out of it.

Trim the right side of the cut-out heart shape with some ready-gathered lace. Place the 2 pieces of cotton fabric right sides together and sew around 3 of the sides. Leave the fourth side open for filling. Turn the sachet the right side out and then fill with dried lavender flowers, leaves and herbs.

Neatly sew along the open edge to finish the sachet and then trim with more of the ready-gathered lace used on the heart shape. Finally, sew or glue on a small bow to decorate the heart.

Mix together a handful of dried tulip petals, marigolds, poppies and rose petals and add 15 ml (1 tbsp) orris root powder.

Add 20 drops of any floral essential oil of your choice and mix well. Cut out 2 pieces of calico 45 cm (18 in) square and join them together, leaving a small gap for filling.

Turn the pillow the right side out, then fill with a mixture of scented pot pourri and polyester cushion filling. Sew along the gap to close the pillow. Cut out 2 pieces of cotton fabric 45 cm (18 in) square, stitch some ribbon and lace across the corners of one piece and then edge the same piece with some cream Cluny lace or any other lace of your choice.

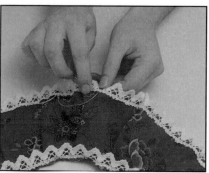

Assuming your fabric to be 1.3 m (4 ft) wide, cut 3 strips 10 cm (4 in) wide and join together along the short edges to make the frill. Edge with lace and gather to fit the pillow. Stitch it to the decorated piece, then cover the seam with lace. Join the 2 pieces together with their right sides facing, leaving a gap for turning. Turn and press. Place the calico pillow inside and sew up the gap.

C ut out a square of lace fabric slightly larger than the diameter of your embroidery hoop. You will also need some brightly coloured pot pourri, ribbons and lace.

Stretch the square of lace fabric across the embroidery hoop and secure it.

Turn the hoop over and fill with pot pourri. Trim any excess lace from the edge of the hoop.

Using a hot glue gun, glue a circle of lace to the back of the hoop and trim to fit exactly. Glue satin ribbon around the edge of the embroidery hoop and glue ready-gathered lace around the back of the frame. Tie a length of ribbon to the screw attachment on the hoop for hanging and then trim with dried flowers and a ribbon bow, using the glue gun to secure them.

TEDDY PINCUSHION

C ut out a 25 cm (10 in) circle of
lace fabric and 20.5 cm (8 in)
circle of cotton or other pretty fabric.
You will also need a small teddy or
doll and some pot pourri.

Stitch the cotton fabric to the lace to
line it. Place lace side down and put
some polyester wadding on top.
Place the teddy on the wadding and
add some pot pourri.

Gather up the lace and fasten off
firmly. Decorate the bear as shown
with lace, beads and ribbon. There
are many variations at this point; use
whatever you happen to have handy
to add to the finished effect. These
trimmings can be sewn on or
attached with a hot glue gun.

—MUSLIN POT POURRI SACHET—

C ut out 2 rectangles of muslin, or another fine fabric, to the required size. You will also need some pot pourri scented with the essential oil of your choice.

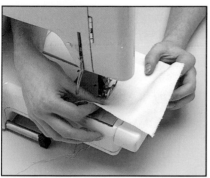

Machine-stitch 3 sides of the rectangle, leaving the fourth side open for turning.

Turn the muslin sachet right sides out and fill with the pot pourri.

Turn under the raw edges of the sachet and oversew by hand. The sachet can be opened and filled with more pot pourri when the existing mixture loses its scent. You can place the sachet inside the oven gloves (see pages 24-5), tea cosy (see pages 26-7), herbal hot mat (see pages 28-9) or inside cushions.

—FRAGRANT OVEN GLOVES—

You will need 2 pieces of washable fabric 1m (40 in) long by 20.5 cm (8 in) wide, 2 pieces of the same fabric measuring 15 x 10 cm (6 x 4 in) and some muslin for the sachets. The herb pot pourri mixture is made from a handful of each of the following: dried mint, marjoram, wormwood and lavender.

Place the herbs in a bowl and add 15 ml (1 tbsp) orris root powder and 10-15 drops of any herbal essential oil of your choice. Mix well.

Make small muslin sachets about 7.5 x 5 cm (3 x 2 in) and fill with the herbal pot pourri (see page 23). Make 2 small pockets from the 15 x 10 cm (6 x 4 in) pieces of fabric and attach to the wrong side of one of the longer pieces, about 5 cm (2 in) from the ends. Stitch both large pieces of fabric, right sides together, leaving a gap for turning.

Turn right sides out and place an 18 cm (7 in) square of wadding inside each end of the mitt, placing them about 15 cm (6 in) from the ends. Stitch through all the thicknesses to secure the wadding and then turn the ends of the mitt over the wadding and stitch. Sew a loop of ribbon in the centre to hang the oven mitt on a hook and place the herb sachets in the small pockets inside the mitts.

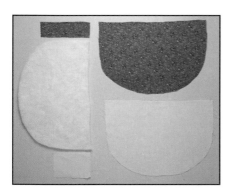

Using the template on page 91, cut out 2 pieces of cotton fabric, 2 pieces of wadding and 2 pieces of calico. You will also need some small pieces of calico and a strip of the cotton fabric.

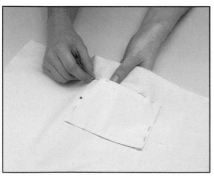

Pin and then stitch a small calico pocket to one of the calico shapes, with its open edge facing the curved top of the calico piece.

Fold the strip of cotton fabric lengthwise, with right sides together, and sew along the long edge. Turn right sides out and press flat.

Fold the strip into a loop and sew, at the centre top, onto the right side of one of the pieces of cotton fabric.

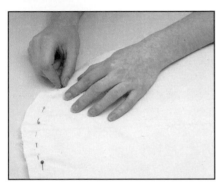

Join each piece of calico to its piece of wadding and stitch in place around the edge.

Stitch the straight edges of the calico pieces and the main fabric pieces together, with right sides together. Open out the calico pieces and the main fabric pieces, and place on top of each other with right sides together. Sew around the edge, leaving a gap for turning in the calico section. Make sure the loop is free and not caught up in the stitching.

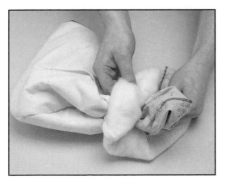

Turn the cosy right sides out and sew up the gap. Press well, then push the lining inside the main coloured piece. Make up a mixture of aromatic spices, such as cinnamon, nutmeg, star anise and allspice, and mix with 5 ml (1 tsp) orris root powder and some allspice essential oil. Place the mixture in small muslin sachets (see page 23) and put in the calico pocket of the tea cosy.

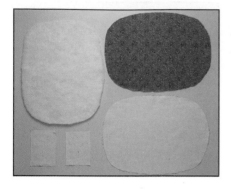

Using the template on page 92, cut out 3 oval shapes 45 cm (18 in) long by 32.5 cm (13 in) wide, one in calico, one in wadding and one in your chosen fabric. Cut out 2 small calico patches to make pockets.

Make the 2 calico pockets and stitch them to the larger piece of calico about 5 cm (2 in) in from the shorter edges.

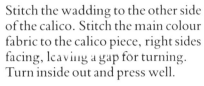

Stitch the wadding to the other side of the calico. Stitch the main colour fabric to the calico piece, right sides facing, leaving a gap for turning. Turn inside out and press well.

Close the gap and then machine stitch all the way around the mat about 0.5cm (¼ in) in from the edge, to give a decorative finish. Make up a mixture of dried herbal flowers and add 5 ml (1 tsp) orris root powder and a few drops of a herbal essential oil. Fill some muslin sachets (see page 23) and place in the calico pockets under the hot mat.

M ake a small bundle of lavender by wiring a few fresh or dried stems together, and attach a narrow satin ribbon bow.

Using a hot glue gun, attach the lavender bundle and bow to a photograph frame.

As a finishing touch, add some dried pink rosebuds, using the hot glue gun.

Take a cleaned and varnished old horseshoe. Using narrow satin ribbon, make a long loop and push one end through the top hole on one side of the horseshoe and tie in a knot. Leaving a long length of ribbon, tie the other end through the top hole on the other side of the horseshoe and tie securely.

Using a hot glue gun, attach some dried *Statice dumosa* (sea lavender) to the horseshoe, to act as a base for the other flowers.

Add dried roses, helichrysum and larkspur to give a really beautiful finished effect.

C ut out a double-layered square of net, fill with pot pourri and tie up with ribbon.

Attach the net bag to a small straw hat, using a hot glue gun.

Attach a satin or other ribbon bow with streamers to the hat. The length of the streamers is up to you.

Glue on some dried sea lavender all around the hat as a base for other dried flowers. Continue to add other flowers; use whatever you have available but remember the flowers need to be small.

—MINIATURE SCENTED BASKET—

P lace some dried flower foam in
a basket and drop on some
essential oil of your choice. Rose
always works well.

Fill the basket with dried sea
lavender, embedded in the flower
foam, and then put in some larkspur.

Add roses and any other flowers you
wish, then trim with bows and
ribbons to tone in with the colour
scheme.

LACY SWEET BAGS

T hese were referred to as sweet bags in the past because of their sweet smell – nothing to do with the edible variety of sweets! Take one cotton lawn, lace-edged handkerchief and place 15 ml (1 tbsp) strongly scented pot pourri in the centre.

Gather up the edges of the handkerchief so that they are all of equal length and secure the bundle with a small elastic band.

Tie a narrow ribbon around the neck and decorate the bag by adding some pink rosebuds or other flowers, using a hot glue gun.

Take some fresh roses, carefully pull off the petals and lay them across a wire rack to dry.

Once you have a sufficient quantity of dried rose petals, place them all in a mixing bowl and add a few drops of rose essential oil to intensify the smell.

Put the rose petal confetti into a clear bag and tie up with ribbons to take to a wedding or give as a wedding gift.

—APPLE AND CINNAMON RING—

D ry apple slices in a conventional oven, on a very low temperature for several hours. For this ring, choose an attractive small twiggy wreath and, using a hot glue gun, attach the apple slices around the ring.

Add some whole or broken cinnamon sticks, securing them with the hot glue gun. If you want to increase the cinnamon scent, drop some essential cinnamon oil onto the apple slices.

As a final touch, make a decorative ribbon bow in the colour you want and attach it to the ring.

ROSEBUD POMANDER

This little rosebud ball is simply lovely. The rosebuds can be obtained from a specialist dried flower supplier or from a shop that sells loose pot pourri. You will need 3 or 4 handfuls of rosebuds, a 7.5 cm (3 in) dried flower foam ball, three 15 cm (6 in) lengths of medium gauge florist's wire, 30–35 cm (12–14 in) lengths of ribbon and one of lace.

Make a loop with the length of lace and wrap a wire around the ends, leaving a leg that is at least 10 cm (4 in) long. Push this wire straight through the foam ball and out the other side. Bend the end over to make a hook and push it back up into the foam to secure it in place. The ribbons can then be wired in the same way, but with shorter legs, and just pushed into the ball.

Take a rosebud and, starting near the point where the ribbon meets the foam ball, press the short stem into the foam. Continue to press in rosebuds, either in a random pattern or in straight lines, until the ball is completely covered. Take care to sort out the rosebuds first, so you use only the best shapes, sizes and colours.

These apple pomanders look lovely piled in a bowl, either amongst fresh fruit or with nuts, or with a selection of other pomanders. You can also make pomanders from lemons, oranges and limes. If you want to hang it up, fix a length of ribbon round the apple and make it into a loop. Take a fresh apple and use a knitting needle to make small holes in it.

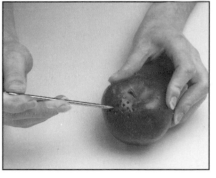

Fill the holes with whole cloves, then continue in this way until you have covered the entire apple.

Roll the finished apple or several apples in a polythene bag containing 15 ml (1 tbsp) orris root powder and 15 ml (1 tbsp) mixed powdered spices, then place the apple pomanders to dry on a warm radiator or in an airing cupboard for several weeks until they are completely dry.

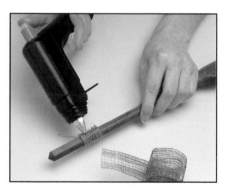

T̄ake a 5 cm (2 in) length of medium gauge florist's wire and bend it in half, into a loop. Glue this loop onto the back of the spoon handle. Wrap a piece of ribbon around the handle to hide the ends of the wire loop and secure with a glue gun.

Glue on a ribbon bow with short or long streamers, depending on your preference.

Using the glue gun, attach some dried flowers to make a decorative spray above and below the bow.

FLOWER WREATH

Choose an attractive twiggy wreath and, using a hot glue gun, attach a large bow, either centre bottom, to one side or wherever you wish on the wreath.

Glue on some dried hydrangea heads, either part of the way around the wreath or all the way round, depending on your preference.

Add some dried achillea (yarrow) and then some helichrysum heads. Obviously the choice of flowers is yours and can be altered to fit any colour scheme or room.

DECORATED BOX

C hoose an attractive box. If it needs recovering this can be done using lining paper and then painting it, or using wrapping paper or wallpaper. Fabric is another possibility, but if you are adding flowers try to keep the fabric as plain as possible. Make wired loops of lace or ribbon and glue them onto the lid of the box with a hot glue gun.

Depending on the size of the box, choose fairly large or special flowers rather than a mass of smaller flowers. Flowers dried in silica gel crystals (see page 9) are ideal for this project. The box illustrated is decorated with peonies, which make a wonderful focal point.

Finish the lid with smaller dried flowers to blend with the lace or ribbon and peonies and soften the arrangement.

—LAVENDER AND ROSE BASKET—

C hoose a basket, then glue a green plastic frog, which holds dried flower foam in place, into the base of the basket. Place a trimmed block of dried flower foam in the basket, impaled on the prongs of the frog. Cover the foam with sea lavender as a base for the other flowers. Then add several bunches of dried lavender: this adds a delightful colour as well as perfume.

Add dried roses of your choice. The ones shown here are a champagne colour and very pretty, but you could also use pink or peach. Roses are well worth drying yourself as they are expensive to buy.

Make double loops with some pretty ribbon and wire the base of each loop. Secure these loops either side of the handles, as a finishing touch.

— WHEAT WITH HYDRANGEAS —

Choose a fairly low basket, either circular or oval. Fill with dried flower foam, then take some wheat, place it in a tight circle and stick the stems into the foam, one at a time. It is important to get the bundle of wheat closely packed and fairly even.

Once you have enough wheat in place, tie a ribbon around the bunch, securing it with a double knot so that it does not slip, then tie in a decorative bow. Alternatively, you can knot a piece of ribbon around the stalks and trim it neatly, then glue on a ready-made bow.

Cover the rest of the foam with dried hydrangea heads so that they form a circle around the wheat. Dried hydrangeas come in many shades, often greens and burgundies, but it is possible to dry the paler blues and pinks.

A basket decorated with silk flowers makes a particularly pretty container for pot pourri or any small gift. Choose your flowers and ribbons to co-ordinate with both the pot pourri going inside the basket as well as the room that the basket is going to be in. Firmly attach the flowers to the edge of the basket, starting wherever you wish.

Make sure the rim of the basket is well covered with flowers so the design is not too sparse. The best glue to use is that from a hot glue gun as any other craft glue takes too long to set and involves a great deal of time spent holding the flowers in position.

When the rim is completely covered, make some ribbon loops in the colour of your choice – these can look very attractive and add a colour that was unavailable in the flowers you used. Attach them to the basket with glue.

-A BOUQUET OF DRIED FLOWERS-

C ollect together the flowers of your choice to include in your bouquet. Lay out the longest ones at the base of the arrangement.

Add some shorter flowers until the bunch is full enough and looks fairly even.

Wind some florist's wire firmly around the base of the stalks to hold them all in position. If some of the smaller ones seem loose, then secure them in place with a hot glue gun. Cover the wire with some pretty ribbon tied into a decorative bow.

Finally, to give added depth to the bunch, add some heavier heads, such as peonies, low down near the bow. It is much easier to glue these on with a hot glue gun than to try wiring them.

Collect together silk flowers and leaves of your choice and a plain greetings card – these can be bought from many craft shops and outlets.

Start by gluing the leaves in a curved design or a 'C' shape on the face of the card. This creates the basic shape of the floral display.

Trim away as much stalk as possible from the flowers so the card is not too bulky, then glue the flowers in position. Pearls or ribbons can be added in small loops to decorate the design, if wished.

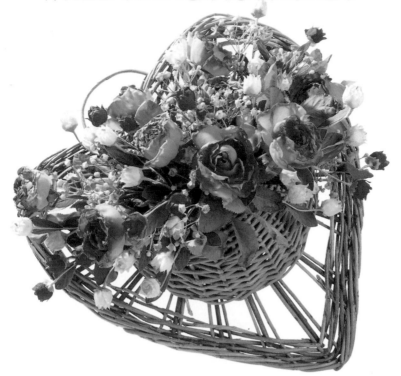

F ill the chosen flat-backed basket
with some dried flower foam,
using a hot glue gun to secure it in
position.

Cover the foam with moss. Reindeer
moss is easily available from craft
shops and gives a good covering
without preventing the stems going
through it.

Arrange the silk flowers of your
choice in the basket, starting with
larger blooms and adding smaller
ones for padding as you go along.
Make sure the basket is attractive
from all angles, particularly from
below, as you will probably be
looking up at the arrangement when
it is on the wall.

—COUNTRY-STYLE STRAW HAT—

This wonderful hat is very easy to make at home, especially if you have a hot glue gun: other types of glue are much weaker and more difficult to use. As well as the hat, you will need a bow, some large silk flowers and leaves and some smaller varieties of silk flowers. This design features silk peonies, larkspur and gypsophila, plus some dried sea lavender.

Glue the ribbon bow on to the centre back of the hat and then attach some sea lavender with the hot glue gun. If you wish to use only silk flowers, as opposed to a mixture of silk and dried ingredients, substitute something similar that would make a good base and fill out the design – some pieces of silk hydrangea heads or a larger quantity of the gypsophila are ideal.

When you are happy with the shape of the basic ingredients around the hat, glue on the largest flowers and some leaves. You can either place these in random groups or symmetrically around the brim. Any full, many-petalled flowers are suitable, such as roses, carnations, gardenias or camellias.

Finally, glue on the smaller, more delicate items, which in this case are larkspur and gypsophila. These finer ingredients fill the brim and add a dainty look which balances well with the larger, more dominant flowers. As a final touch you could scent the hat by dropping some essential oil onto the flowers.

- TABLE CENTRE ARRANGEMENT -

When creating a table centre arrangement, it is important not to make it too tall as this can obstruct people's view of those opposite and tends to dominate the table. Choose a fairly low basket and fill with dried flower foam or use a piece of cork as a base and place the foam on top. Cover the foam with moss to make sure it is completely hidden.

Place the silk leaves you are using in position first. They should make an oval shape if the arrangement is intended for a rectangular or oval table, or a circle if it is meant for a square or circular table. In this arrangement small artificial pears have been used to give an added interesting feature.

Lastly, add the flowers. When using silk flowers there is a vast and unlimited choice of flowers from all seasons and all climates but it makes an arrangement more realistic if you can use flowers from just one season. Spring and autumn flowers mixed together will immediately give away the secret that you have used silk flowers.

A silk posy makes a pretty gift for someone who is unwell. Posy holders can be purchased from florists and craft shops and make the task of making posies far easier. Begin by covering the foam in the posy holder with a selection of silk leaves to form the base of the posy. This not only covers the green foam base but also helps to pad out the display.

Add the flowers, starting with smaller blooms and then adding the larger items. In this case, the roses are the main features of the posy. A variety of shapes and forms adds to the interest of the bouquet.

Make sure that the back of the posy looks neat and professionally finished. If necessary, add some extra leaves to cover any untidy stalks, then decorate the stem of the posy holder with ribbons tied into bows.

This summery combination of poppies, wheat and cornflowers looks wonderful in a rustic wicker hamper. You could use an ordinary basket if a small hamper is not easily available. Fill the hamper with a large piece of dried flower foam.

Cover the foam with dried hydrangea heads to camouflage it. You could use moss or some sea lavender if preferred.

Add some dried wheat, making sure the stems are inserted at pleasing angles and do not all rigidly point towards the sky. This arrangement needs quite a lot of wheat to pad out the display and give a good contrast to the red silk poppies. Alternatively, some dried achillea (yarrow) and dried poppy seed heads can be used, as shown here.

Place some silk poppies in position next and lastly add some silk or dried cornflowers. Add ribbons, or a ribbon bow, if wished.

Any basket would be suitable for this project but the lighter and daintier it is the better; sweet peas are not large overpowering flowers and a heavy rustic basket might not work quite as well. Start by one handle and glue on the silk flowers and leaves, making them look as natural as possible.

A hot glue gun is essential as speed is of the essence when attaching the flowers to the handle. Continue adding flowers, making them look as though they were growing up the handle. In this case the tendrils add a really natural and realistic touch. Glue bows on either side of the handle.

As this is such an open weave basket a lining is useful, and in this case a Nottingham lace handkerchief is placed in the basket together with bubble bath pearls and some dried rosebuds.

Take a blank piece of card and, using tweezers, arrange some dried leaves on it (in this case maidenhair fern), then add some dried pink larkspur and some grasses.

Carefully stick down all the leaves and flowers with some latex adhesive, applying it with a needle or piece of florist's wire, then cover the design with a piece of clear film.

To scent the bookmark, place it with some pot pourri in a box and cover. Leave for a few weeks to take up the smell of the pot pourri.

─ FRAGRANT WRITING PAPER ─

A rrange a small design on the outside flap of the envelopes and also on one corner of the sheets of notepaper. You may like to leave some sheets blank for continuation sheets.

Glue the pressed flowers and leaves firmly in place with latex adhesive, applying it with a needle or piece of florist's wire, and then cover with a piece of clear film.

Leave the paper and envelopes in a large box with some highly scented pot pourri for a few weeks, then tie the sheets of paper with a toning ribbon and place in their presentation box.

U se a piece of firm card and arrange pressed leaves in an oval, leaving spaces for flowers to be added.

Tuck in a selection of flowers and dainty fillers – in this case, alchemilla and roses – then glue firmly with latex adhesive, applying it with a needle or piece of florist's wire.

Place in any frame of your choice, making sure the glass is clean and that the back of the picture is well sealed.

U sing either a piece of card folded to size or a ready-made blank greetings card, arrange a pretty design on it with pressed flowers and leaves.

Glue the arrangement firmly with latex adhesive, applying it with a needle or piece of florist's wire, and then cover carefully with a piece of clear film.

Place the card and its envelope in a box with highly scented rose petals, or some rose-scented pot pourri, and leave it for a few weeks until the card has taken up the rose fragrance.

—DECORATED PHOTO FRAME—

U se a pre-cut photograph mount – or use the template on page 93 – and arrange some pressed leaves around the opening.

Add some more pressed flowers and other pieces to fill out the design.

Glue them carefully in position with latex adhesive, applying it with a needle or piece of florist's wire, and then tap the mount gently to make sure all the pieces are firmly attached. Place the mount in the frame and attach the photograph.

— A SPECIAL WEDDING CARD —

U se a plain piece of card or a specially made blank greetings card. In this case the card has a silver edge. Arrange some pressed leaves on the card to begin the design.

Add some pressed fern and some red roses or other flowers of your choice. Finish the design with a dainty filler such as gypsophila.

Glue the flowers and leaves carefully with some latex adhesive, applying it with a needle or piece of florist's wire, and then cover the design with a piece of clear film.

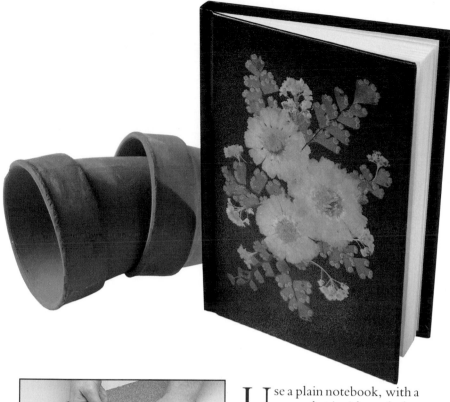

U se a plain notebook, with a cover that is either a dark colour or very pale, such as cream or white. Arrange some pressed leaves on the front to start the design.

Add some pressed flowers, using fairly bright colours if they are against a dark background, to make a strong contrast.

Carefully stick down the flowers and leaves with latex adhesive, applying it with a needle or piece of florist's wire, and then cover with a piece of clear film.

DECORATED CINNAMON STICKS

Take 5 cinnamon sticks and glue them together in a bundle, using a hot glue gun.

Wrap a ribbon around the bundle of cinnamon sticks and tie in a decorative bow.

Glue on some dried sea lavender, with the flowers flowing along the bundle rather than across it. Add any other dried flowers you wish. If you want to increase the cinnamon scent, drop a little cinnamon essential oil onto the decoration.

Use whole bay leaves, which can either be gathered from a bush in your own garden, or that of a neighbour, or bought in a jar intended for culinary purposes. Paint over both sides of the leaves with gold paint.

To create different finishes, use several different golds or a bronze or copper colour. Allow the leaves to dry on an old cake cooling rack.

Having wrapped up your parcel, attach the gilded leaves with a hot glue gun and add some nuts or dried flowers.

─── AROMATIC SPICE POSY ───

Using medium to fine gauge florist's wire, attach lengths of wire to several cones and spices, such as star anise, cinnamon or tiny alder cones and beech masts.

Starting with a larger item, such as a single helichrysum flower, make a posy shape around this central feature. Wrap the stems together with florist's tape.

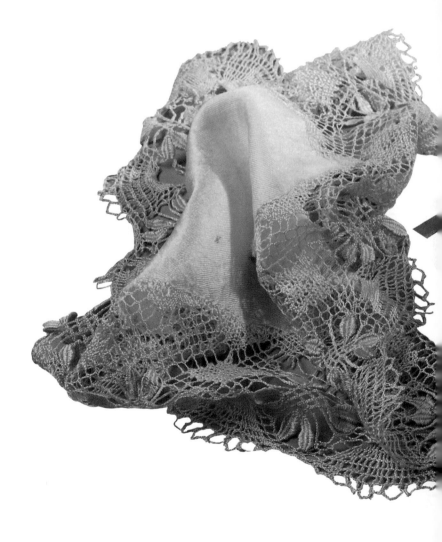

Keep adding to the posy, firmly wrapping the stem of each new ingredient with tape. Tie a ribbon bow at the base of the posy.

Place the posy in a small posy holder and cover the stems with ribbon in the same colour as the bow.

-APPLE AND HERB DECORATION-

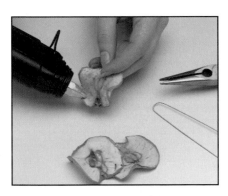

You will need some slices of dried apple, some wire and a selection of small dried flowers, beech masts and some ribbon. Glue the apple slices together to make a circle.

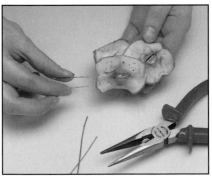

Thread some florist's wire through the top of your circle to make a hanging loop. Twist the wire firmly to secure it.

Decorate with the flowers or beech masts and glue on a couple of ribbon bows, in this case one in green and one in gold.

—CHRISTMAS TREE WALNUTS—

D rill 2 small holes through the top of each walnut and thread through a length of gold cord.

Using a hot glue gun, add some small alder cones in a group on the top of each walnut.

Finish the decoration with small sprigs of dried sea lavender. To scent the decoration, sprinkle a couple of drops of pot pourri essential oil onto the cones.

Half-fill a flower pot with plaster of Paris or cement and embed a stick in the middle. The stick should be approximately 35 cm (14 in) long, depending on your required finished height. Once the cement is dry, cover with dry flower foam and arrange some sea lavender to cover the foam.

Place a nail through the stick about 2.5 cm (1 in) down from the top and impale a dry flower foam ball onto the stick, with the nail going into the ball.

Cover the ball with sea lavender until the grey foam is barely visible.

Add more dried flowers of your choice in a suitably festive colour, in this case red helichrysum and green *Nigella orientalis*. Make a long loop with some tartan ribbon, attach it to some florist's wire and stick this into the foam ball where the stick (tree trunk) meets the ball.

Finally add some more ribbon loops to the base and some more of the same flowers you used in the top half of the tree.

Y ou will need 60 cm (24 in) red
felt and a strip of white fur 49
cm (19½ in) long and 7 cm (2¾ in)
wide. You will also need some red
ribbon to make a hanging loop.
Cut the red felt into a stocking shape,
using the stocking-shaped template
on page 94.

Carefully pin the strip of fur along
the top edge of the felt stocking.

Machine (or hand-sew) the fur onto
the felt. Sew on a ribbon loop for
hanging, then sew up the front and
foot part of the stocking.

Using a hot glue gun, attach some
spruce, pine cones, dried
gypsophila and Christmas tree bells
to the stocking. Finally sew on a
ribbon bow.

—— A CHRISTMAS NUT BALL ——

T ake a pre-formed sphere of dried
flower foam. Make a long loop
with some ribbon and twist a
reasonably long length of wire
around the base of the loop, leaving a
'leg' to go through the ball. Pass the
wire through the ball until the base of
the loop is embedded in the foam.
Trim the wire to within 1 cm (½ in)
and bend it back into the foam.

Using a hot glue gun, glue a selection
of nuts onto the foam, being fairly
liberal with the glue.

Once the ball is completely covered
with nuts, check for glimpses of the
grey foam and, if there are any, cover
them with some dried nigella seed
heads. Spray the ball well with a
polyurethane matt or satin varnish.

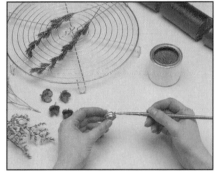

Assemble some gilded nigella heads, grasses, dried sea lavender and beech masts or cones. You will also need some gold ribbon or cord. Either make a plain cracker of your own or use a sparsely decorated bought one.

Using a hot glue gun, attach the ingredients to one side of the cracker.

Once you are happy with the design, add some tiny loops of gold ribbon or cord, making sure that the base of each loop is well hidden.

—CHRISTMAS NAPKIN RINGS—

Y ou will need some plain wooden napkin rings, a selection of dried flowers and cones, gilded wheat and some gold ribbon or cord.

Using a hot glue gun, attach the longer pieces from your choice of flowers and cones – in this case the gilded wheat. Then add some flowers until you are happy with the design.

Make some small loops with the gold ribbon and glue them into the arrangement, being careful that the base of each loop does not show.

C ollect some scented rose petals from the garden and wash them well. Dry carefully with tissues and lay out on a cake cooling rack to dry.

Once they are dry, store them in the box or container you wish to give them in as a present and gradually add to them.

Decorate the box or container with some dried flowers, ribbon and perhaps a label. To make rose petal tea, pour 300 ml (½ pint) boiling water over 10 ml (1 dessertspoon) rose petals and allow to stand, then strain well. Elderflowers can be used instead of rose petals if you prefer.

──── ROSE PETAL SALAD OIL ────

C hoose an attractive container to fill with oil. Measure how much oil it will hold, then add 30 ml (2 tbsp) dried rose petals per 600 ml (1 pint) oil.

Using a funnel, pour the oil – sunflower or rapeseed works well – over the rose petals. Leave to mature for a couple of days, shaking occasionally.

Decorate the container before giving it as a present, using some dainty rose-coloured ribbon.

—CARNATION VINEGAR—

F ill the base of a pretty glass container with dried carnation heads.

Add white wine or cider vinegar, filling the container to the top.

Seal the top and then decorate the container with some pretty ribbons.

Y ou will need some dried
lavender, a funnel, white wine
or cider vinegar, a suitable container
and some ribbon.

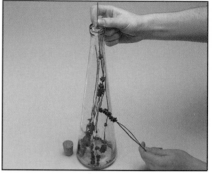

Place some lavender stalks in the
container with their heads pointing
downwards. Fill up the container
with the vinegar.

Seal the top and then decorate the
bottle with a spray of lavender and
some ribbons.

MARIGOLD MUSTARD

Finely chop some dried marigold flowers. You will need 20 ml (2 dessertspoons) for a 225 g (8 oz) pot of mustard. It is best to use a strong, grainy mustard.

Mix the chopped marigolds into the mustard, making sure they are well distributed.

Spoon the marigold mustard into a sealable container, seal it, then decorate with a suitable bow or other decoration. This mustard is excellent with cold pork.

— LAVENDER HONEY —

Warm a pot of runny honey, plus a handful of lavender flowers, in a heatproof bowl over a saucepan of gently simmering water. Do not allow the honey to boil, just gently warm it through with the lavender for about 15 minutes.

Strain the honey through a fine sieve and discard the lavender flowers.

Pour the honey into an attractive container and place a sprig of lavender in the top. Seal the container and then decorate it with a small bunch of lavender and some ribbons.

—A FLOWER-COVERED BOW—

You will need a fabric bow mounted onto a hairslide, some dried flowers and some wired pearls.

Using a hot glue gun, stick on a selection of dried flowers, including sea lavender, either side of the knot in the bow.

Finally, make loops of pearls, securing them with wire. Add the loops and some individual pearls to finish the bow.

A CHILD'S SWEET PEA HAIRBAND

Y ou will need a couple of sprays of silk sweet pea flowers with some foliage and tendrils, a plastic hairband and some ribbon.

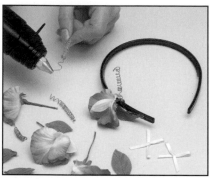

Separate the sweet pea flowers and leaves from their stalks or sprays. Individually attach each leaf and flower to the hairband, using a hot glue gun.

Ensure you add some tendrils as they make a huge difference to the finished design. Add a ribbon bow at each end of the hairband in a toning colour.

CARNATION COMBS

You will need 1 or 2 side combs, some silk spray carnations and some leaves, gold cord, wired pearls and some reel wire.

Using a hot glue gun, first attach the leaves to the comb(s) and then the silk carnations.

Make small wired loops with the gold cord or ribbon and glue these on to the comb(s), then as a finishing touch add some small wired pearls.

ORCHID SIDE COMBS

Y ou will need 2 tortoiseshell hair combs and some silk orchids with leaves.

Separate the blooms and leaves from the orchid spray, then attach some leaves to one of the combs, using a hot glue gun.

Glue a couple of flowers onto the comb. Repeat the operation with the second comb to make a matching pair.

Y ou will need some silk rosebuds and some tortoiseshell hairslides.

Separate the rosebuds and leaves. Using a hot glue gun attach the leaves to the hairslides in an attractive pattern.

Add the rosebuds; you can use all the same colour or alternate between 2 different colours.

──ROSE AND PEARL COMB──

Collect together a clear or pearlized side comb, some dried and scented rosebuds, some gypsophila, a length of pearls and some reel wire.

Make some loops with the pearl string and the reel wire. Attach these to each end of the comb.

In the centre of the comb, glue on a cluster of the fragrant rosebuds, using a hot glue gun, and add some dainty sprigs of gypsophila.

ROSE HAIRSLIDE

You will need a large gilt hairslide, 3 dried rose heads, sea lavender, gypsophila and gold cord or ribbon. First attach the sea lavender and 3 roses to the hairslide, using a hot glue gun.

Make some tiny loops with the ribbon and glue those deep into the design.

Finish the slide by adding dainty sprigs of gypsophila to lighten the overall effect.

The design templates on the following pages are printed on 1–cm (⅜–in) grids to help you copy them more easily. To reproduce the design, draw up a grid making the squares the same, double or three times the size they are here, according to the size you wish your project to be. Copy the design, one square at a time, on to your grid. When completed, you can cut it out and use it like an ordinary paper pattern.

LAVENDER AND HERB SACHET
(pages 16-17)

SCENTED TEA COSY
(pages 26-7)

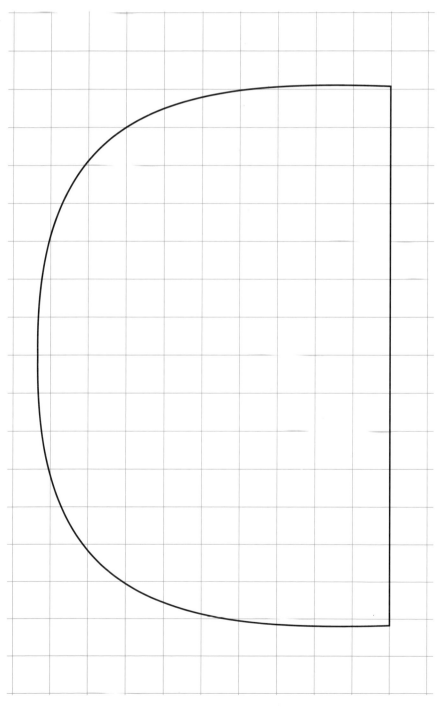

HERBAL HOT MAT
(pages 28-9)

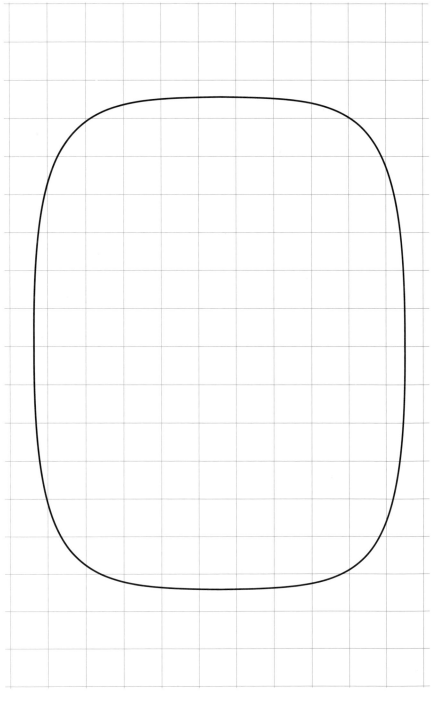

DECORATED PHOTO FRAME
(page 61)

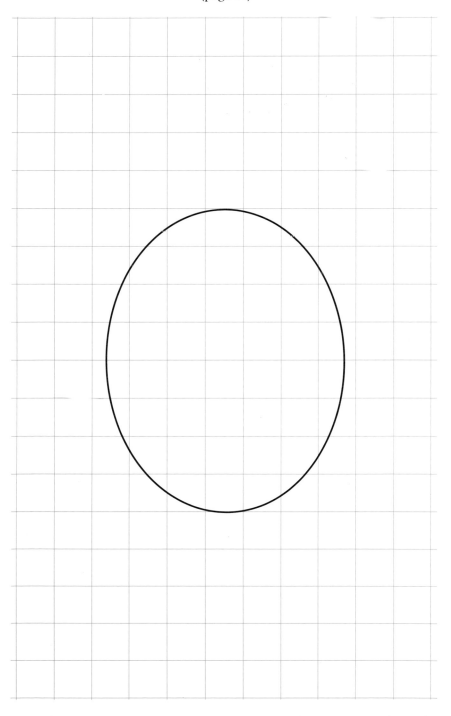

CHRISTMAS STOCKING
(page 72)

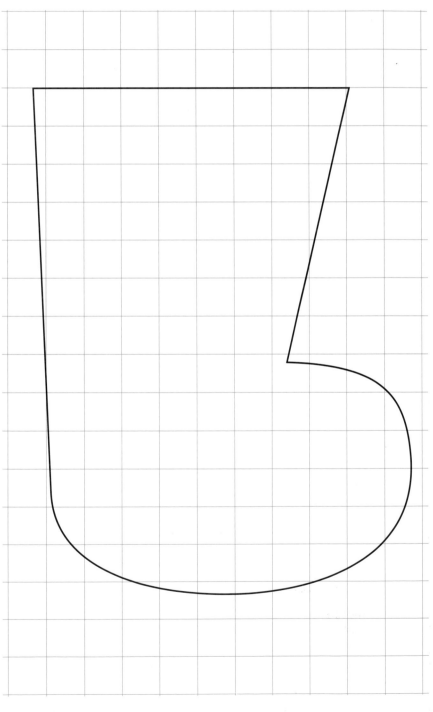

INDEX

SUPPLIERS

Pressed flower equipment, dried flowers and some pot pourri ingredients and other craft items:
Joanna Sheen Limited, PO Box 52, Newton Abbot, Devon TQ12 4YF

General flower arranging equipment, silica crystals and some pot pourri ingredients:
The Diddybox, 132–134 Belmont Road, Astley Bridge, Bolton, Lancashire BL1 7AN

Pot pourri ingredients:
G Baldwin and Co, 173 Walworth Road, London SE17 1RW